Deutscher Iaido Bund e.V. (ed.)

Visualization of the examination criteria
ZNKR-Iai
(Chakuganten)

Idea and implementation of Rudi Müller
Illustrations by Leona Dürhager

Visualization of the examination criteria ZNKR-Iai
(Chakuganten)

Idea and implementation of Rudi Müller
Illustrations by Leona Dürhager
Deutscher Iaido Bund e.V. (ed.)

Bibliografische Information der Deutschen Nationalbibliothek: Die Deutsche Nationalbibliothek verzeichnet diese Publikation in der Deutschen Nationalbibliografie; detaillierte bibliografische Daten sind im Internet über http://dnb.dnb.de abrufbar.

Die automatisierte Analyse des Werkes, um daraus Informationen insbesondere über Muster, Trends und Korrelationen gemäß §44b UrhG („Text und Data Mining") zu gewinnen, ist untersagt.

Idee und Umsetzung: Rudi Müller
Illustrationen: Leona Dürhager
Umsetzung für den Buchdruck: Ralf Bonnekoh

Verlag: BoD · Books on Demand GmbH, In de Tarpen 42, 22848 Norderstedt, bod@bod.de

Druck: Libri Plureos GmbH, Friedensallee 273, 22763 Hamburg

ISBN: 978-3-7693-2455-6

CONTENTS

Foreword

"A picture is worth a thousand words" is a 100-year-old saying attributed to a Japanese philosopher.

The text of the examination criteria is not easy to read, which is not surprising when translated from Japanese. If you translate it literally, hardly anyone will understand what is meant; if you translate it freely, you run the risk of moving away from the actual meaning.

The idea of visualizing the so-called chakuganten, or what we call examination criteria, came about. At a glance (or two), you can grasp the essential criteria.

There are certainly a lot of other topics beyond the 40 examination criteria listed on the 4 pages of the Zen Ken Ren Iai commentary. But that should not be used as an excuse not to appreciate and learn the examination criteria accordingly. The committee members of the Zen Nihon Kendō Renmei certainly had their valid reasons for adding these points as an addition.

Even though our Japanese teachers tell us every summer that some techniques have changed, it is now clear to all high grades that this does not affect the validity of the Zen Ken Ren Iai commentary. Changes are intended to counteract undesirable developments, minimize dangerous techniques or simplify movement sequences for beginners.

The following graphics are intended solely to make it easier to learn the examination criteria. This booklet cannot replace lessons. Individual points (a, b, c, etc.) sometimes contain two or three pieces of information. This is why we worked with sub-points (a1, a2, etc.) which are assigned to a graphic.

I now hope that all Iaidōka, whether candidates or competitors, and especially all instructors, examiners and competition judges, find it easier for them to internalize the examination criteria with this booklet.

Yours

Rudi Müller

Iaidō kyōshi 7th dan

Words of thanks

My very special thanks go to the artist of these beautiful graphics and her perseverance and patience when asked to make the umpteenth improvement - Leona Dürhager from Steinbach.

Thanks also to the board of the DIaiB, in particular vice president, Ralf Bonnekoh, for his openness to the project and the financial and marketing support.

Finally, I would like to thank my two committee members, Sylvia Ordynsky, kyōshi 7th dan and Wim van Mourik, renshi 6th dan for their commitment to the proofreading.

Stegaurach, July 1st, 2024

Rudi Müller,

Iaidō kyōshi 7th dan

The assessment of the Zen Nihon Kendō Renmei Iai

The examination criteria

Sahō (reihō)

Is the specified manner of etiquette performed? *(See the German translation of Zen Ken Ren Iai commentary on pages 17 to 25.)*

1. form mae

a)   When drawing, is enough sayabiki performed?
b)   Is the katana raised over the head with the feeling as if one is thrusting backwards along the left ear?
c)   When lifting the sword over the head, does the kissaki not hang lower than the horizontal?
d)   Is the downward cut made without a pause?
e)   Is the kissaki a little lower (than the horizontal) after the downward cut?
f)   Is the general tendency of chiburi correct?
g)   Is nōtō performed correctly?

2. form ushiro

a)   While the examinee turns, is the katana drawn at the same time; is the left foot placed forcefully to the left?
b)   Is it pulled through the opponent's temple correctly?

3. form ukenagashi

a)   Is the upper body brought into a protected posture in the ukenagashi position?
b)   Is the left foot pulled back towards the right foot and a kesa cut made?
c)   If the left fist stops in front of the belly button, is the kissaki slightly lower (than horizontal)?

4. form tsukaate

a)   Does the tsukagashira hit the opponent's suigetsu exactly?
b)   If the right elbow is extended when thrusting the opponent behind, does the left hand turn and press the koiguchi, which is still held, in front of the belly button?
c)   Is the front opponent cut straight forward while the katana is pulled (from the opponent) and raised above the head?

5. form kesagiri

a)   When cutting kesa in reverse and turning the katana, is the right fist above the right shoulder?
b)   Is a chiburi made through the kesa while simultaneously pulling the left foot back and the left hand grasping the koiguchi?

6. form morotetsuki

a)   Is cutting to the chin when drawn diagonally to the right through the opponent's head?
b)   While bringing the katana into chūdan and the back foot to the front, is the suigetsu then thrusted with accuracy?
c)   When drawing (from the opponent) is the katana taken over the head in the ukenagashi manner? (See footnote 46 in the German translation of Zen Ken Ren Iai commentary on page 39.)

7. form sanpōgiri

a)   Is cutting to the chin when drawn to the right opponent?
b)   Does the examinee turn to the opponent on the left and is cut without a pause from straight forward downwards?
c)   After the katana has been taken over the head and cut in the ukenagashi manner (see footnote 46 in the German translation of Zen Ken Ren Iai commentary on page 39), is the katana in a horizontal position?

8. form ganmenate

a)   Is the tsukagashira correctly used to strike between the eyes?
b)   Is the right fist correctly placed on the right hip (above the hip bone) opposite the opponent behind?
c)   Has the examinee turned completely to the opponent behind, is the left heel slightly raised when thrusting?
d)   Is the thrusting performed from a straight (literally: not L-shaped) position of the feet?

9. form soetetsuki

a)   When the examinee has cut through the right kesa, is the right fist at the level of the belly button, is the kissaki slightly higher than the right fist?
b)   Is the left hand in the middle of the blade? Is the blade clamped between the thumb and index finger and is the right fist on the right hip? (Above the right hip bone.)
c)   When thrusting into the stomach, does the right fist stop in front of the belly button?
d)   If the right elbow is stretched (literally: not bent) during zanshin, is the right fist not higher than the right side of the chest?

10. form shihōgiri

a)   At tsukaate, is the strike made strongly and precisely with the broad side of the handle?
b)   After sayabiki, is the area of the monouchi placed on the left side of the chest and thrusted precisely to the suigetsu?
c)   When thrusting, is the koiguchi still held and brought in front of the navel and can the examinee completely turn the left hand?
d)   Is the katana moved over the head performing waki no kamae?

11. form sōgiri

a)   When the katana is drawn up and swung out, is this done using the ukenagashi method?
b)   When cutting, is okuriashi (moving the front foot forward and immediately letting the back foot follow) performed?
c)   When the hip/stomach area is cut, is the hasuji (line of the cutting edge, cutting line) correctly horizontal?

12. form nukiuchi

a)   After the katana has been drawn up, is the left foot sufficiently set back?
b)   After the katana has been drawn up, is the position of the right hand in the (body) center line?

a)   When drawing, is enough sayabiki performed?

b)   Is the katana raised over the head with the feeling
as if one is thrusting backwards along the left ear?

c)   When lifting the sword over the head,
does the kissaki not hang lower than the horizontal?

d)   Is the downward cut made without a pause?

e)   Is the kissaki a little lower *(than the horizontal)*
after the downward cut?

f)   Is the general tendency of chiburi correct?

g)   Is nōtō performed correctly?

a)
b)
c)
c)
Pause
d)
e)
f)
g)

a)

    a1)   While the examinee turns,

            is the katana drawn at the same time;

    b)   Is it pulled through the opponent's temple correctly?

a2)   is the left foot placed forcefully to the left?

a)

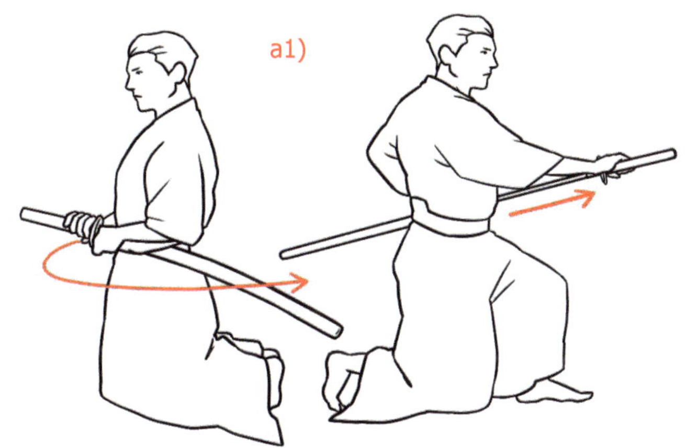

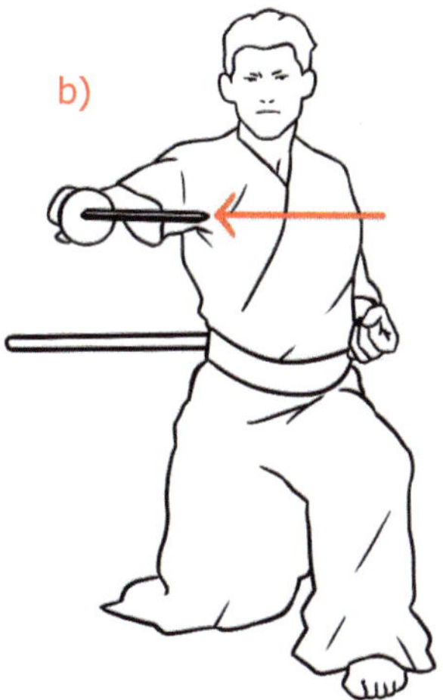

a)   Is the upper body brought into a protected posture

in the ukenagashi position?

b)

b1)   Is the left foot pulled back towards the right foot

(see 1-2-3)

b2)   and a kesa cut made?

c)   If the left fist stops in front of the belly button,

is the kissaki slightly lower *(than horizontal)*?

a)
b)
b1)
b2)
c)
shōmen
kasōteki
1
2
3

a) Does the tsukagashira hit the opponent's suigetsu exactly?

b)

    b1) If the right elbow is extended

        when thrusting the opponent behind,

    b2) turn and press the koiguchi, which is still held,

        in front of the belly button?

c) Is the front opponent cut straight forward,

    while the katana is pulled *(from the opponent)*

    and raised above the head?

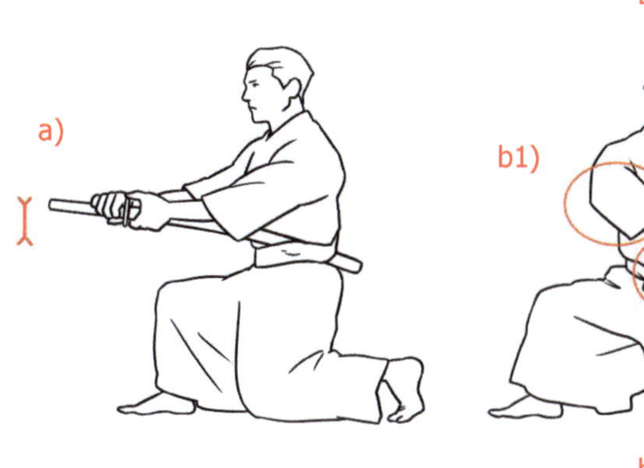

a)
b)
b1)
b2)

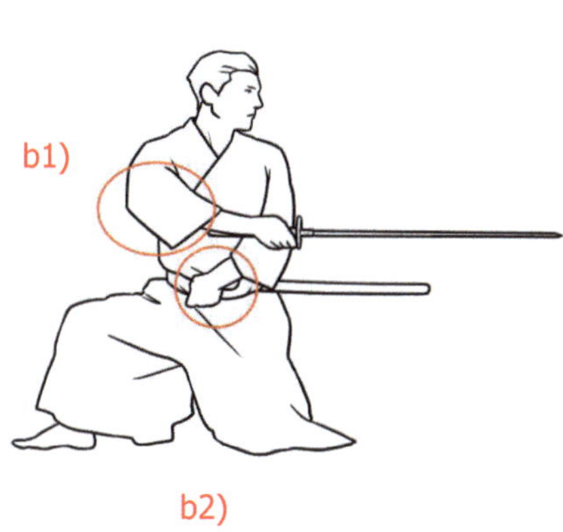

c)

a)

a1)   When cutting kesa in reverse

and turning the katana,

a2)   is the right fist above the right shoulder?

b)

b1)   Is a chiburi made through the kesa,

b2)   while simultaneously pulling the left foot back
and the left hand grasping the koiguchi?

a)

a1)
a2)

b)

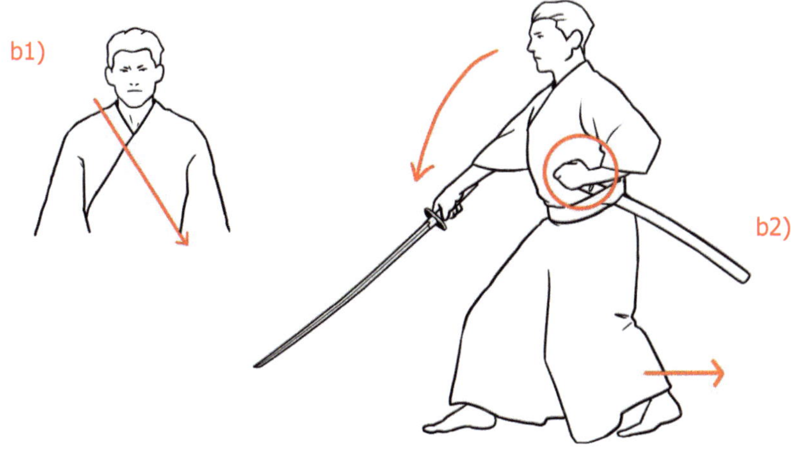
b1)
b2)

a) *a1)*   Is cutting to the chin,

      a2)   when drawn diagonally to the right

              through the opponent's head?

b) *b1)*   While bringing the katana into chūdan

              and the back foot to the front,

      b2)   is the suigetsu then thrusted with accuracy?

c)   When drawing *(from the opponent)* is the katana taken over the head in the ukenagashi manner?

(see footnote 46 in the German translation of the Zen Ken Ren Iai commentary on page 39.)

a)
a1)
a2)
b)
b1)
b2)
c)

a)   Is cutting to the chin when drawn to the right opponent?

b)

  b1)   Does the examinee turn to the opponent on the left
and is cut without a pause

  b2)   straight forward downwards ?

c)

  c1)   After the katana has been taken over the head
and cut in the ukenagashi manner
*(see footnote 46 in the German translation of
the Zen Ken Ren Iai commentary on page 39),*

  c2)   is the katana in a horizontal position?

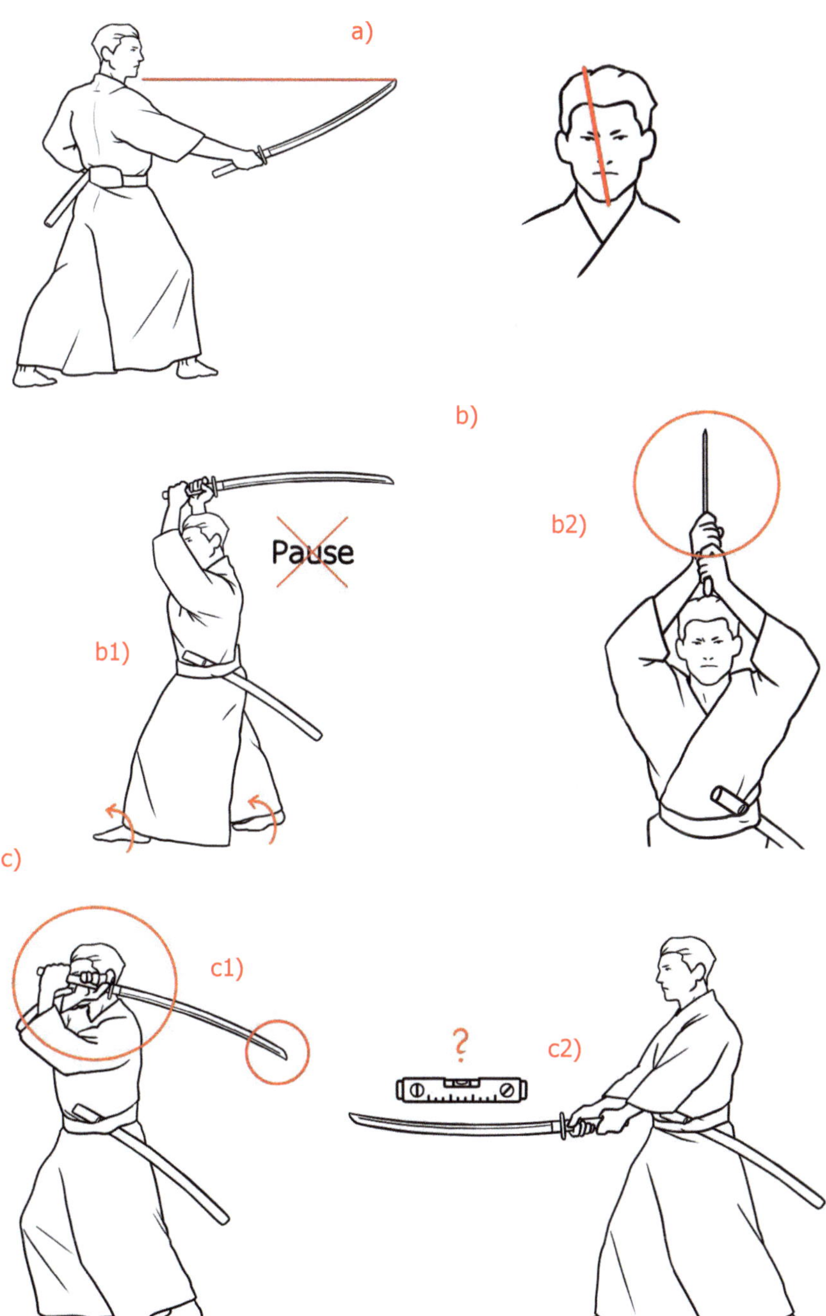
a)
b)
b1)
Pause
b2)
c)
c1)
c2)
?

a)   Is the tsukagashira correctly used to strike between the eyes?

b)   Is the right fist correctly placed on the right hip *(above the hip bone)* opposite the opponent behind?

c)   Has the examinee turned completely to the opponent behind, is the left heel slightly raised when thrusting?

d)   Is the thrusting performed from a straight *(literally: not L-shaped)* position of the feet?

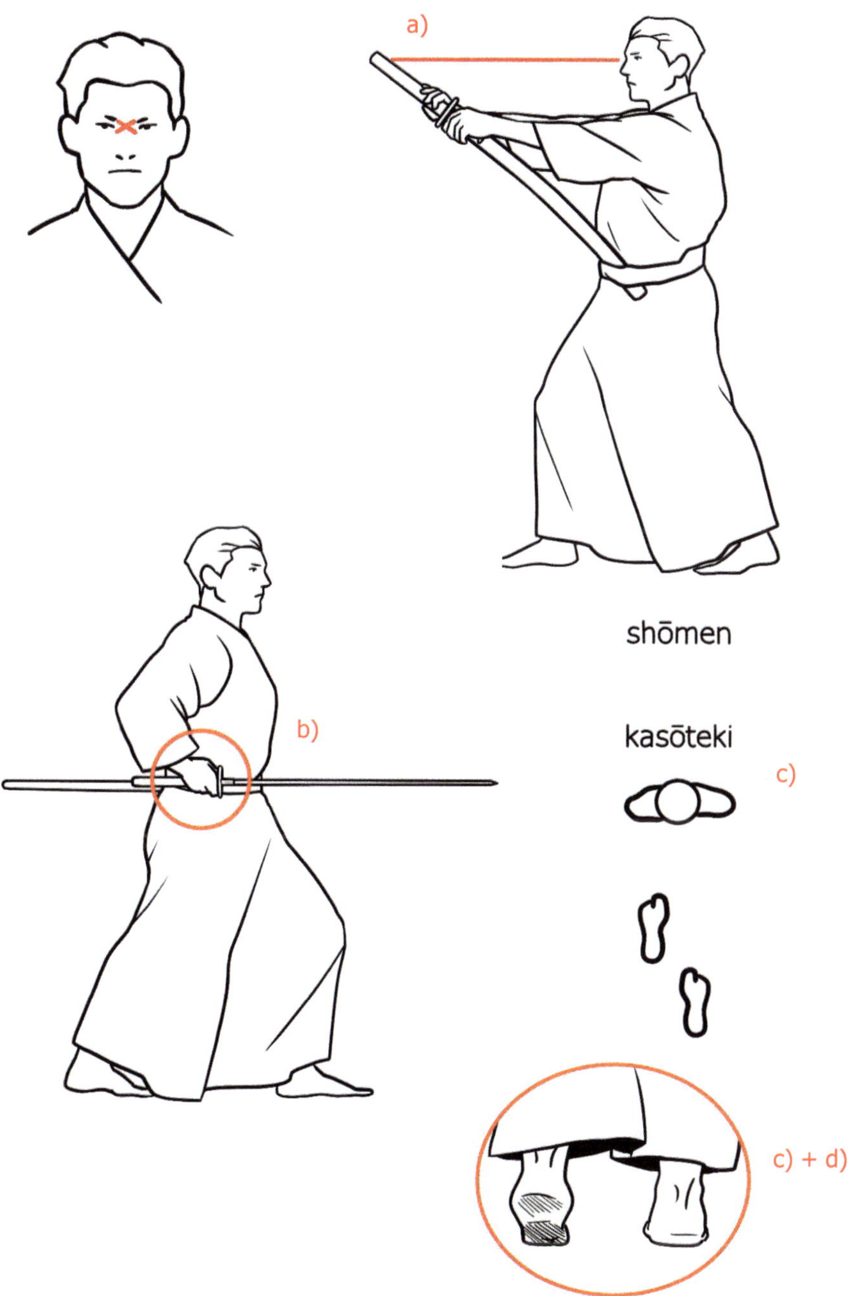

a)
b)
c)
c) + d)
shōmen
kasōteki

a)

> *a1)* When the examinee has cut through the right kesa,

> *a2)* is the right fist at the level of the belly button,
>
> is the kissaki slightly higher than the right fist?

b)

> *b1)* Is the left hand in the middle of the blade?
>
> *b2)* Is the blade clamped between the thumb and index finger
>
> *b3)* and is the right fist on the right hip?
>
> *(Above the right hip bone.)*

c) When thrusting into the stomach,

> does the right fist stop in front of the belly button?

d) If the right elbow stretched *(literally: not bent)* during zanshin,

> is the right fist not higher than the right side of the chest?

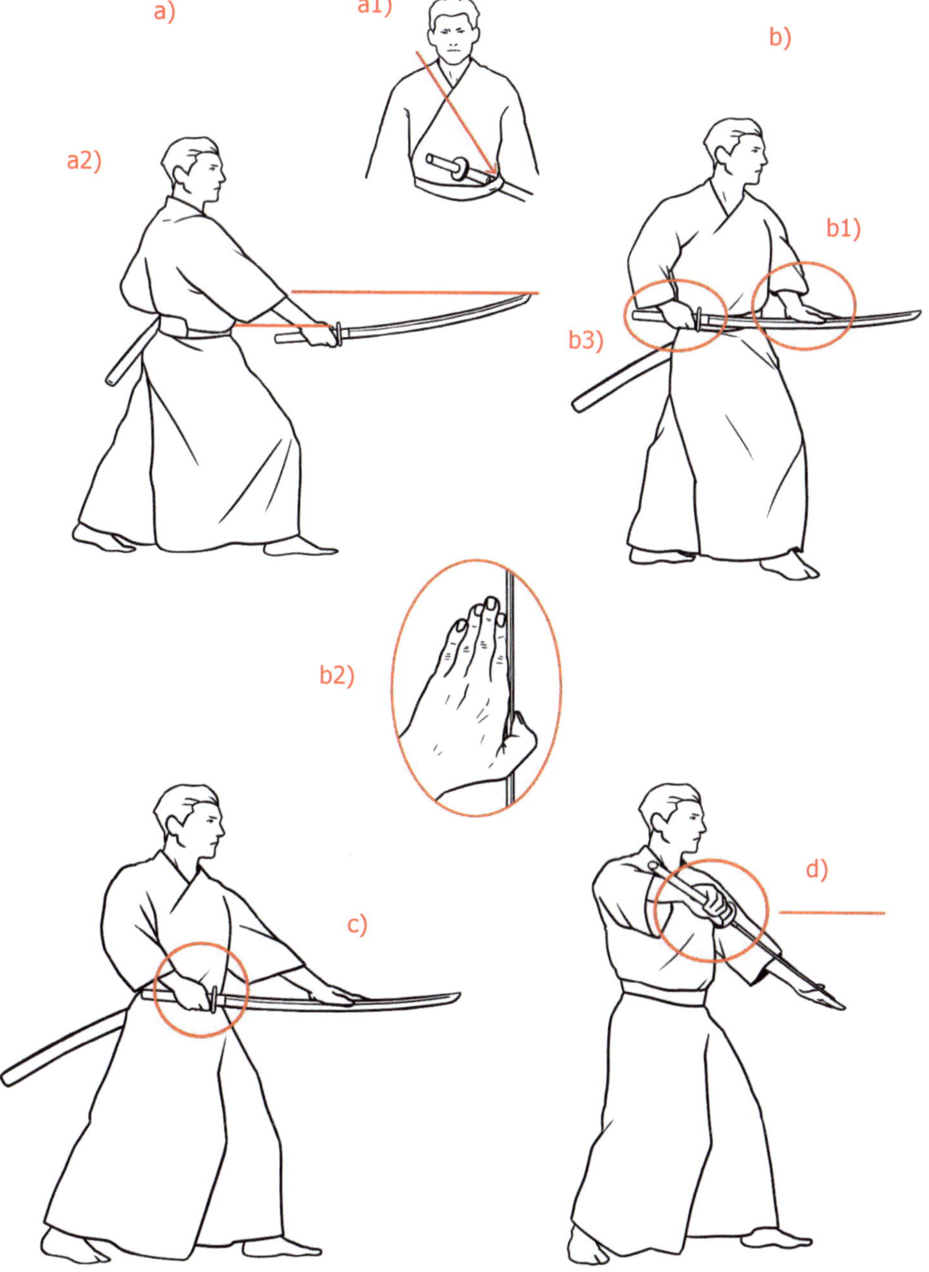

a)
a1)
a2)
b)
b1)
b2)
b3)
c)
d)

a) At tsukaate, is the strike made strongly and precisely

with the broad side of the handle?

b)

b1) After sayabiki, is the area of the monouchi placed

on the left side of the chest

b2) and thrusted precisely to the suigetsu?

c) When thrusting, is the koiguchi still held

and brought in front of the navel

and can the examinee completely turn the left hand?

d) Is the katana moved over the head

after going through waki no kamae?

a)

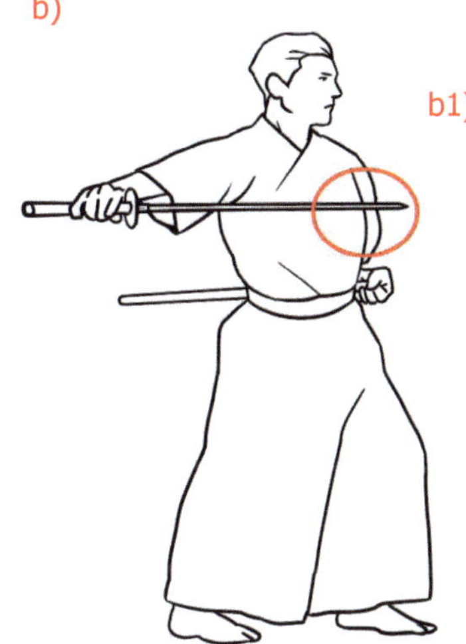
b)
b1)

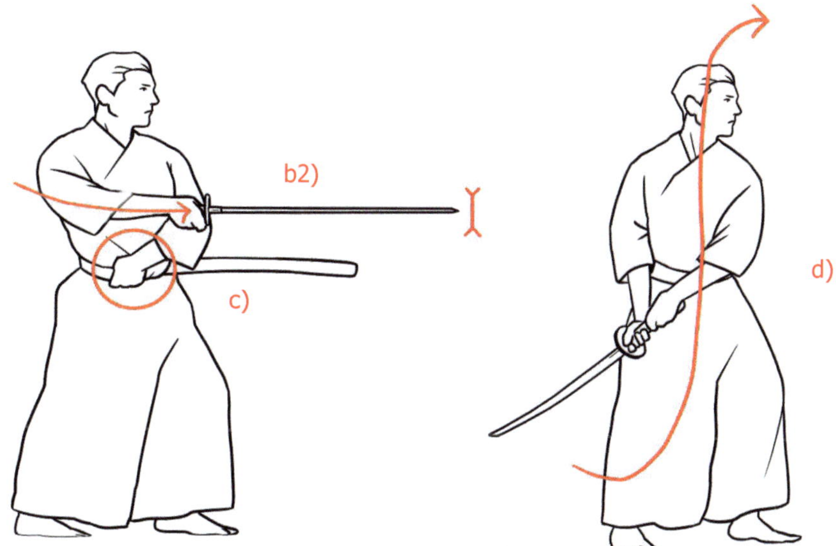
b2)
c)
d)

a)   When the katana is drawn up and swung out,

is this done using the ukenagashi method?

b)   When cutting, is okuriashi *(moving the front foot forward and immediately letting the back foot follow)* performed?

c)   When the hip/stomach area is cut,

is the hasuji *(line of the cutting edge, cutting line)* correctly

horizontal?

a)
b)
c)
?
12
11
10
9
8
7
6
5
4
3
2
1

a)   After the katana has been drawn up,
          is the left foot sufficiently set back?

b)   After the katana has been drawn up,
     is the position of the right hand in the (body) centre line?

a)

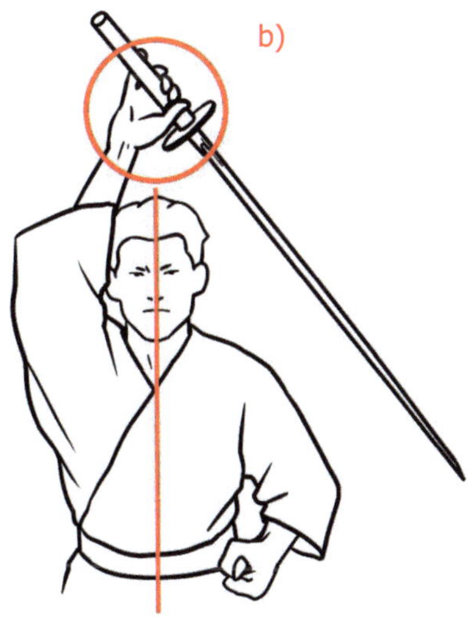

b)